At the back of this book:

Tennessee Reading and Writing Accomplishments

Reading Street

Tennessee

Program Authors

Peter Afflerbach
Camille Blachowicz
Candy Dawson Boyd
Wendy Cheyney
Connie Juel
Edward Kame'enui
Donald Leu
Jeanne Paratore
P. David Pearson
Sam Sebesta
Deborah Simmons
Sharon Vaughn
Susan Watts-Taffe
Karen Kring Wixson

PEARSON
Scott Foresman

Editorial Offices: Glenview, Illinois • Parsippany, New Jersey • New York, New York
Sales Offices: Boston, Massachusetts • Duluth, Georgia • Glenview, Illinois
Coppell, Texas • Sacramento, California • Mesa, Arizona

We dedicate Reading Street to
Peter Jovanovich.

His wisdom, courage,
and passion for education
are an inspiration to us all.

About the Cover Artist

Daniel Moreton lives in New York City, where he uses his computer to create illustrations for books. When he is not working, Daniel enjoys cooking, watching movies, and traveling. On a trip to Mexico, Daniel was inspired by all of the bright colors around him. He likes to use those colors in his art.

ISBN: 0-328-26117-3

2 3 4 5 6 7 8 9 10 V063 15 14 13 12 11 10 09 08 07

Dear Tennessee Reader,

As you continue your trip down *Scott Foresman Reading Street,* you will learn about yourself and others. And, you will improve your reading skills as you travel along!

What changes have you experienced as you have grown? What changes have you noticed in the world around you? The stories and articles in this book are all about changes.

Take time to enjoy yourself and the changes all around you as you continue along *Scott Foresman Reading Street!*

Sincerely,
The Authors

Contents

Read It ONLINE
sfsuccessnet.com

What is changing in our world?

Growing and Changing

Changes in Nature

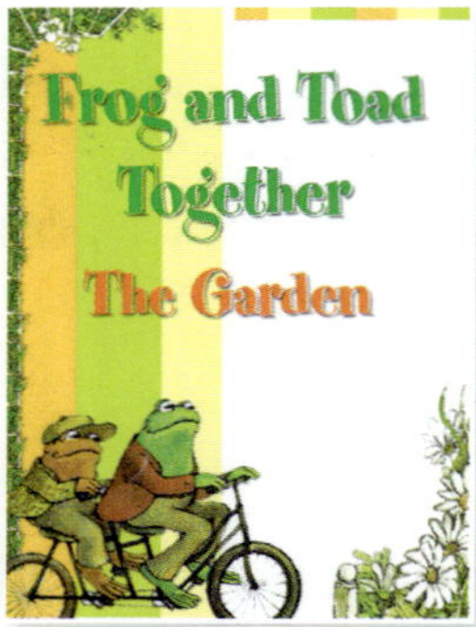

UNIT 3

Changes

What is changing in our world?

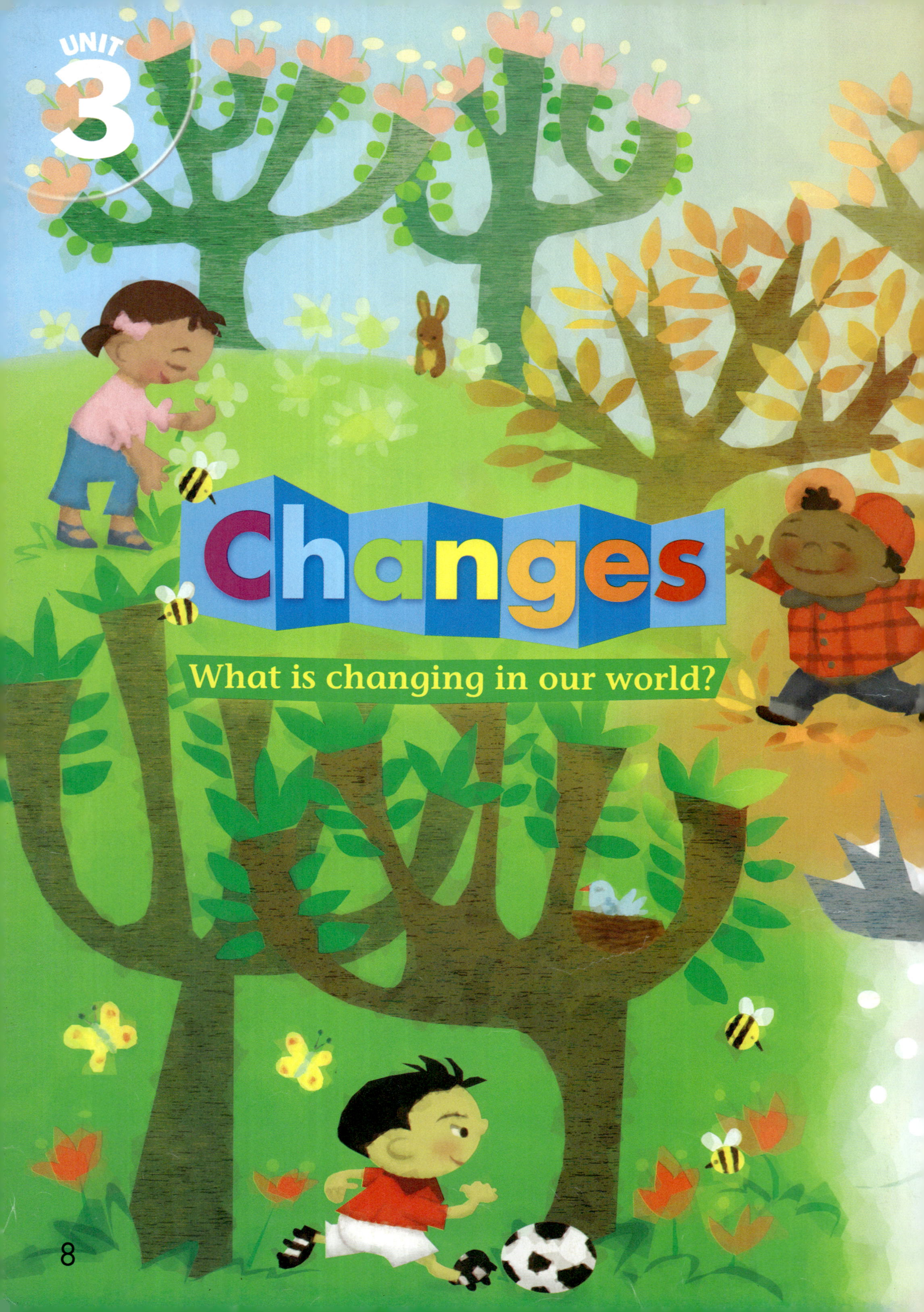

connect to SCIENCE

An Egg Is an Egg

A boy describes changes in our world.

REALISTIC FICTION

connect to SOCIAL STUDIES

Ruby in Her Own Time

A young duckling grows and learns.

ANIMAL FANTASY

connect to SOCIAL STUDIES

Jan's New Home

Moving is a difficult change for Jan.

REALISTIC FICTION

connect to SCIENCE

Frog and Toad Together

Toad sees his garden grow and change.

ANIMAL FANTASY

connect to SCIENCE

I'm a Caterpillar

A caterpillar changes to a butterfly.

NARRATIVE NONFICTION

connect to SCIENCE

Where Are My Animal Friends?

The seasons bring many changes to the forest.

PLAY

Let's Talk About Growing and Changing

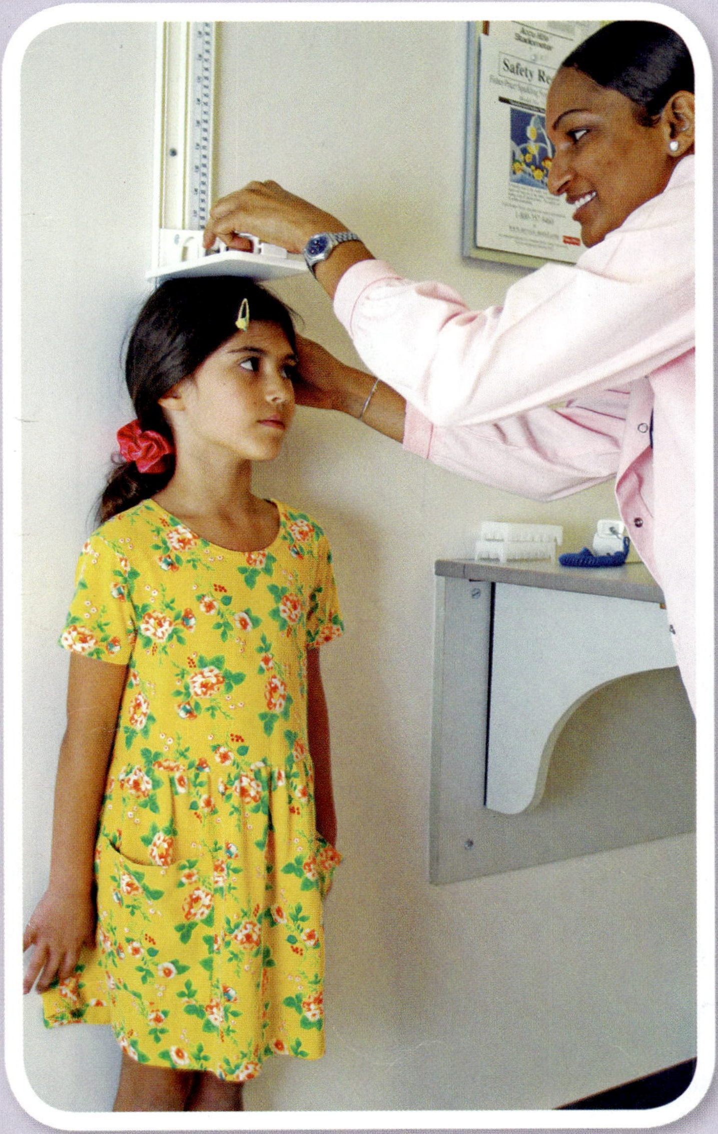

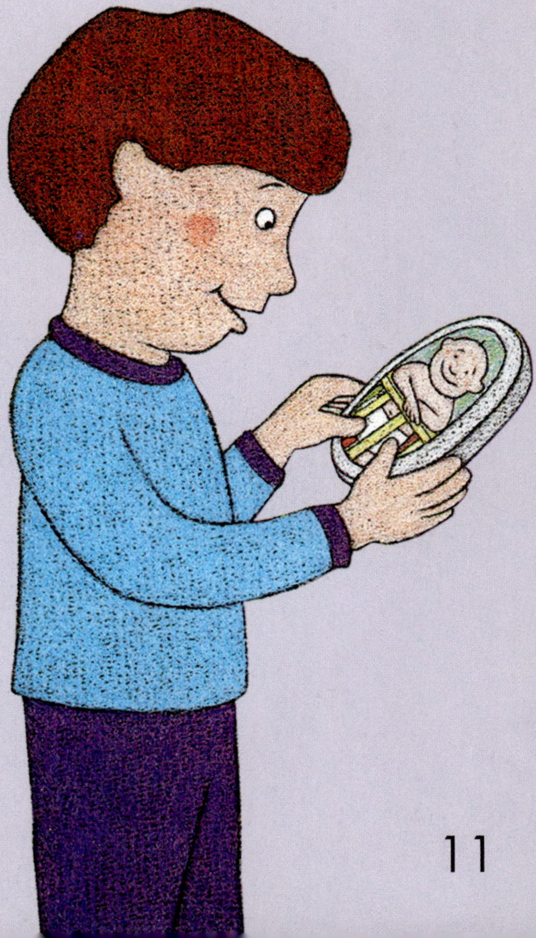

Words to Read

things
always
day
become
nothing
stays
everything

Read the Words

Some things always change. They change from day to day. Children get bigger. Seeds become plants. Nothing stays the same. Everything changes.

Genre: Realistic Fiction
Realistic fiction has characters that act like real people. In *An Egg Is an Egg,* you will read about changes that take place in our world.

An Egg Is an Egg

by Nicki Weiss

When is an egg not an egg?

An egg is an egg until it hatches.
And then it is a chick.

A branch is a branch until it breaks.
And then it is a stick.

Nothing stays the same.
Everything can change.

A seed is a seed until it is sown.
And then it is a flower.

A block is a block until there are many.
And then they become a tower.

Nothing stays the same.
Everything can change.

Water is water until it is brewed.
And then it becomes tea.

You are you until I come.
And then you become "we."

Nothing stays the same.
Everything can change.

The yard is green until it snows.
And then it becomes white.

Day is day until sunset.
And then it is the night.

Nothing stays the same.
Everything can change.

This baby was a baby until he grew.
And now he is a boy.

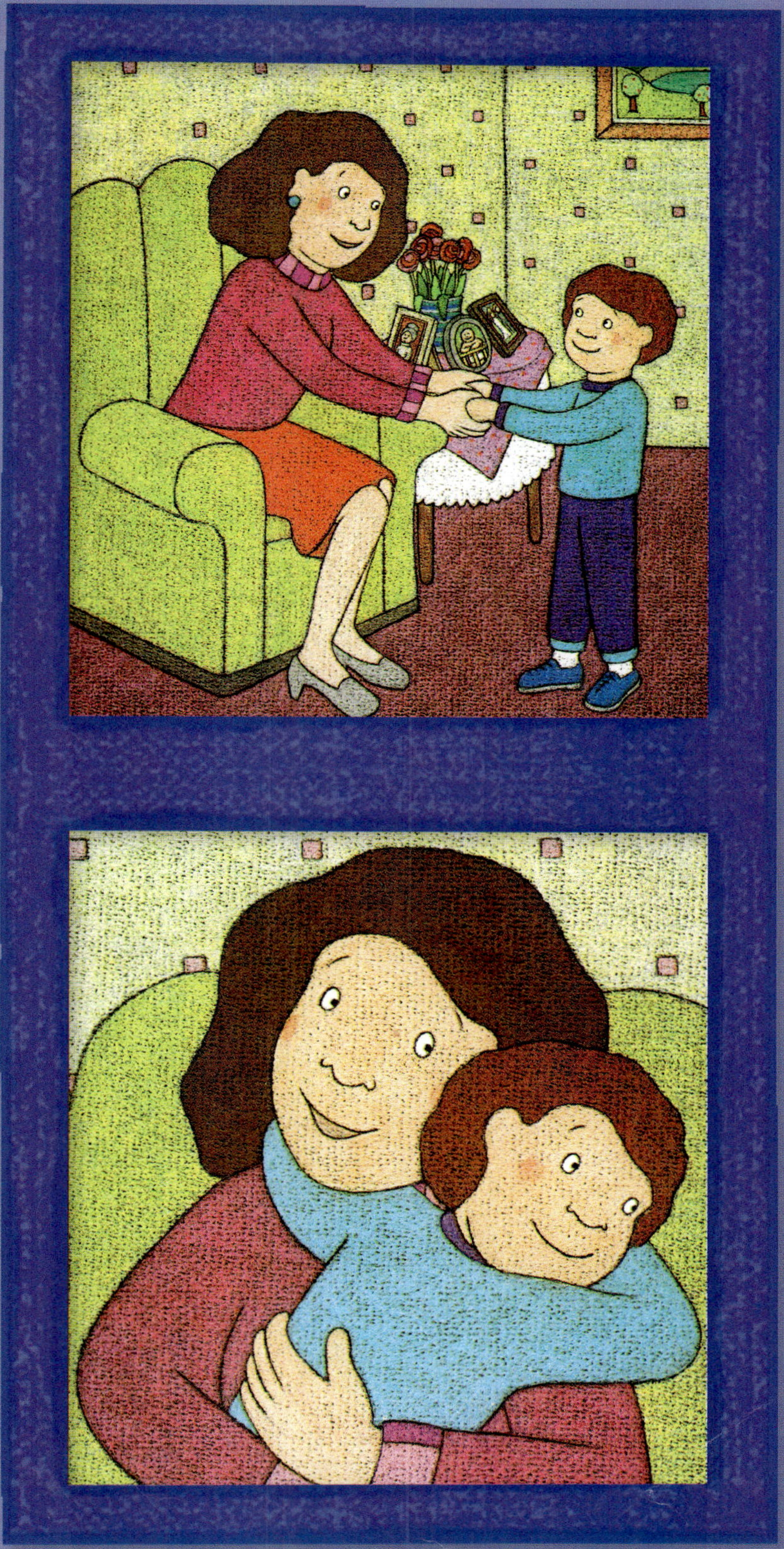

But you can always be a baby.
You will always be my baby. . . .

Some things stay the same.
Some things never change.

Read Together

Think and Share

Talk About It Which change in *An Egg Is an Egg* is your favorite? Tell about it.

1. Use the pictures below to retell the story.
2. Choose a pair of pictures from the story. Tell how they are alike and different.
3. This selection has a pattern that repeats. Did you predict how the yard would change? What helped you?

Look Back and Write Look back at page 25. Write about one thing that does not change.

Meet the Author and Illustrator

Nicki Weiss

Nicki Weiss is an artist, a writer, and a teacher. Her books are about friends, family love, and changes in life.

Ms. Weiss lives in New York City. She wrote lots of books. Then she decided to become a schoolteacher. Now she teaches reading and art. She still writes books when she has the time.

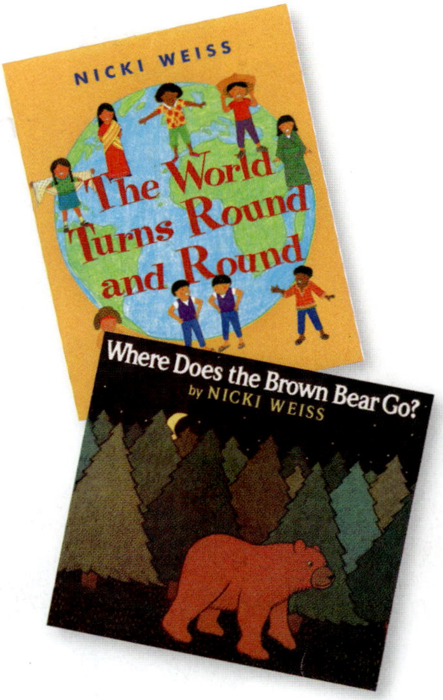

Read more books by Nicki Weiss.

Nothing Fits!

by Rena Moran

illustrated by Mary Bono

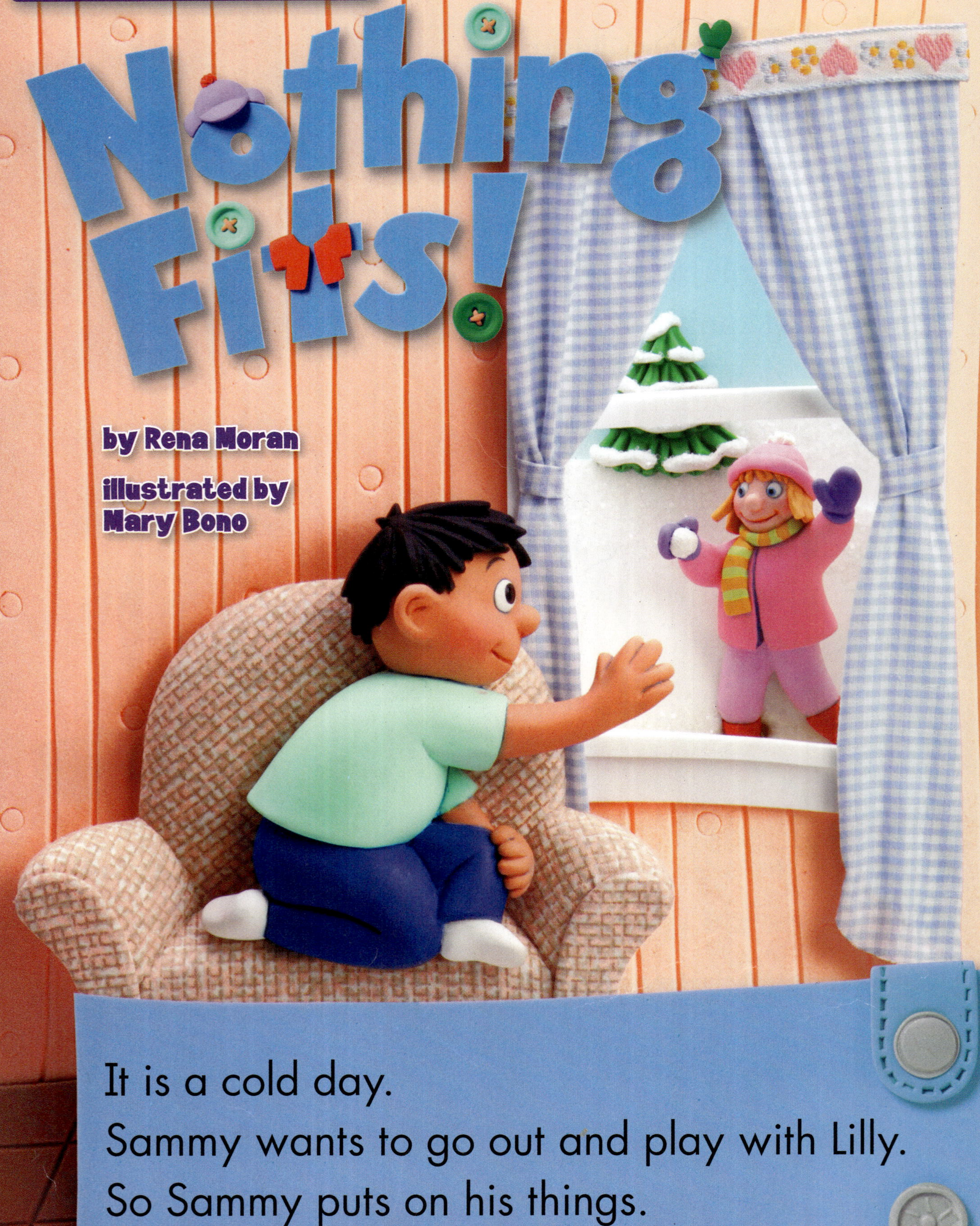

It is a cold day.
Sammy wants to go out and play with Lilly.
So Sammy puts on his things.

Sammy looks silly!
Nothing fits him.
Everything is too small.
Sammy grew.

Dad has new things for Sammy.
He must try them on.
Everything fits!
Sammy will not have to stay inside.

Sammy will keep growing.
He will become a big boy.
But he will always be Sammy.

Read Together

Action Verbs

A **verb** can tell what someone or something does.

Mom **plants** seeds.

The word **plants** tells what Mom does.

The seeds **grow.**

The word **grow** tells what the seeds do.

Write Using Action Verbs

1. Write these sentences. Circle the action verb in each sentence.

Mom drinks her tea.
The boy looks at his picture.

2. Write a sentence about something that happens when a season changes. Circle the action verb.

3. Write some sentences about how a tree changes from summer to fall and from fall to winter. Use action verbs. Circle them.

Let's Talk About Growing and Changing

4 years
5 years
6 years

Words to Read

ever
sure
were
enough
every
any
own

Read the Words

"Have you ever seen this cute duck family in the pond?" asked Ben.

"Sure," said Jill. "They were here last week. I had seeds to feed them then, but not enough for every little duck. Now I don't have any seeds."

"They will have to get their own food," said Ben.

Genre: Animal Fantasy
An animal fantasy is a story with animal characters that talk. Next you will read about a growing duck family.

Ruby in Her Own Time

by Jonathan Emmett

illustrated by Rebecca Harry

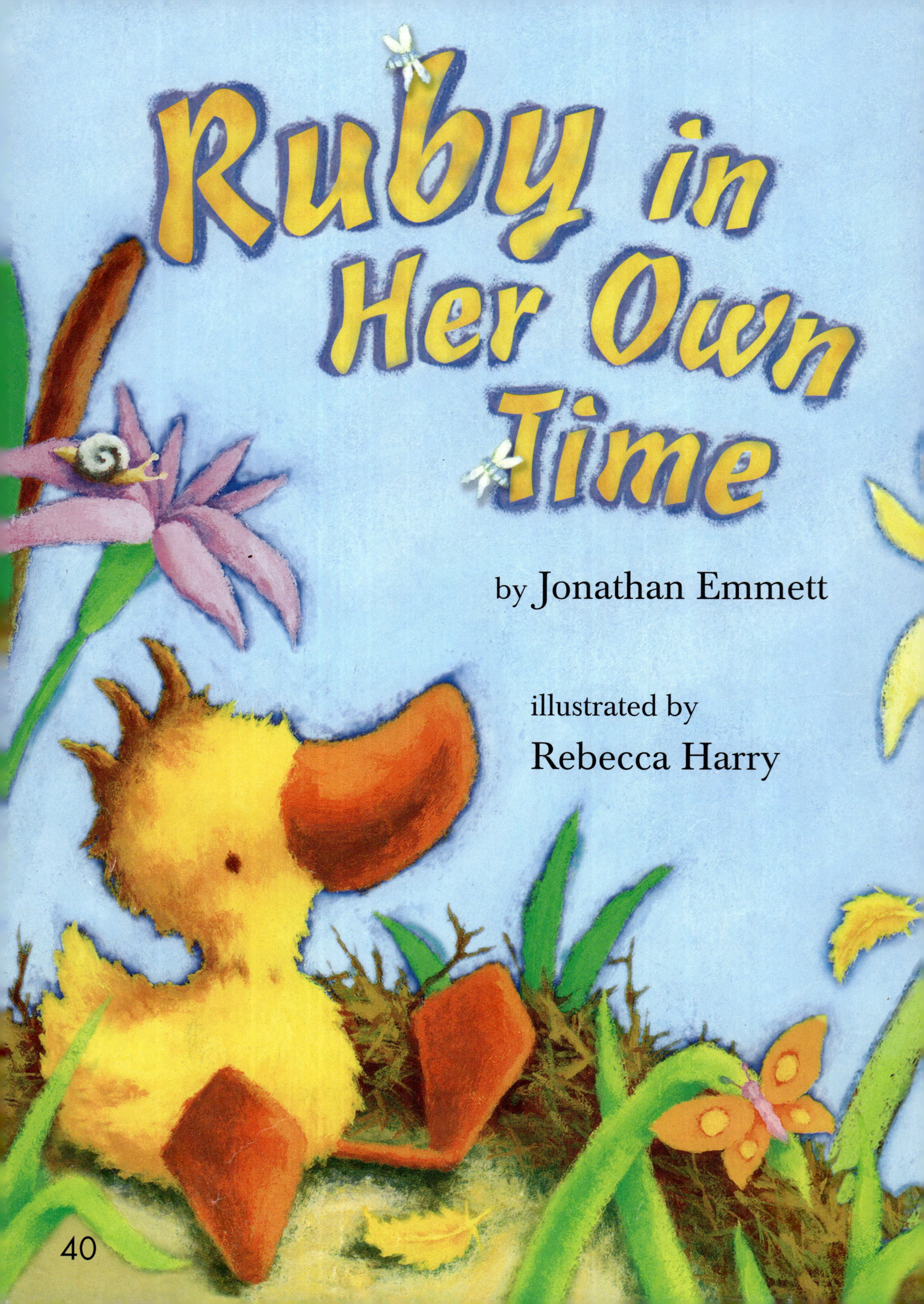

What will Ruby
learn as she grows?

Once upon a time upon a nest beside a lake, there lived two ducks–a mother duck and a father duck.

There were five eggs in the nest. Mother Duck sat upon the nest, all day and all night . . .

through howling wind and driving rain, looking after the eggs–all five of them.

Then, one bright morning,
the eggs began to hatch.

One, two, three, four
little beaks poked out
into the sunlight.

One, two, three, four little ducklings shook their feathers in the breeze.

“We’ll call them Rufus, Rory, Rosie, and Rebecca,” said Father Duck. And Mother Duck agreed.

But the fifth egg did nothing.
"Will it ever hatch?" said Father Duck.

"It will," said Mother Duck,
"in its own time."

And–
sure enough–
it did.

"She's very small," said Father Duck.
"What shall we call her?"

"We'll call her Ruby," said Mother Duck,
"because she's small and precious."

Rufus, Rory, Rosie, and Rebecca ate whatever they were given. They ate anything and everything.

But Ruby ate nothing.

"Will she ever eat?" said Father Duck.

"She will," said Mother
Duck, "in her own time."

And–
sure enough–
she did.

Rufus, Rory, Rosie, and Rebecca swam off whenever they were able.

They swam anywhere and everywhere.

But Ruby swam nowhere.

"Will she ever swim?" said Father Duck.

"She will," said Mother Duck,
"in her own time."

And–
sure enough–
she did.

Rufus, Rory, Rosie, and
Rebecca grew bigger.

And Ruby grew bigger too.
Her feathers grew out, and her
wings grew broad and beautiful.

And when Rufus, Rory, Rosie,
and Rebecca began to fly . . .

Ruby flew too!

Rufus, Rory, Rosie, and Rebecca flew far and wide. They flew out across the water. They flew up among the trees.

But Ruby flew farther and wider. She flew out beyond the water.

She flew up above the trees.

She flew anywhere and everywhere. She stretched out her beautiful wings and soared high among the clouds.

Mother Duck and Father Duck watched Ruby flying off into the distance.

“Will she ever come back?” said Mother Duck.

“She will,” said Father Duck, “in her own time.”

And–
sure enough–
she did.

Read Together

Think and Share

Talk About It What surprised you at the end of the story? Tell about it.

1. Use the pictures below to retell the order in which things happen in this story.
2. What do you think was the most exciting part of this story?
3. Sum up how Ruby grew and changed.

Look Back and Write Look back at page 47. Why did Mother Duck name her baby duck *Ruby?* Write about it.

Meet the Author

Jonathan Emmett

Jonathan Emmett got the idea for this story while jogging around a lake one morning. He saw a swan's nest, and the words "Once upon a time, upon a nest" popped into his head. He changed the swans to ducks, "and the story grew from there."

Mr. Emmett lives in England with his wife and two children.

Read more books by Jonathan Emmett.

I'm Growing

When I was a baby, I couldn't do anything on my own. Mom and Dad sure were a big help!

Then, every day I could do new things. Look at what things I could do. Here's my list.

What I could do	When I did it
Walk	1 year
Talk	2 years
Sing a song	3 years
Brush teeth	4 years
Play catch with a mitt	5 years
Ride a two-wheel bike	6 years

When I am old enough, I could fly a plane!
Do you ever think of what you will do?

Read Together

Verbs That Add -s

A **verb** can tell what one person, animal, or thing does. Add an **-s** to show what is being done now.

Ruby **swims** in the pond.

Ruby is one duck, so we add **-s** to the word **swim.**

Write Using Verbs That Add -s

1. Write these sentences. Use the correct form of the verb.

Rory (eat, eats) her food.
Mother Duck (see, sees) Ruby fly.

2. Write a sentence that tells the sound one duck makes. Circle the verb.

3. Write a list of sentences that tell what one duck does. Circle the verbs that add **-s.**

Build Background

Let's Talk About

Growing and Changing

SCHOOL BU
Kitchen
KITCHEN
DISHES
KITCHEN
Books

Words to Read

very
car
away
our
house
school
friends

Read the Words

Jan was very sad. As her family drove off in the car, she said, "I don't want to go away. I like our house. I like my school and my friends. Let's stay here."

Genre: Realistic Fiction
Realistic fiction is a made-up story about things that could really happen. The next story is about a girl who must move to a new home.

Jan's New Home

by Angela Shelf Medearis

illustrated by Don Tate

What will change when Jan moves to a new home?

Jan and her family must move away.
Jan is sad. She wants to stay.

Our house, our school,
our friends will change.
But Jan wishes everything
could stay the same.

Jan puts her things away in a box.
She packs her toys, her dresses, her socks.

Boxes, boxes here and there!
Boxes of things are everywhere!

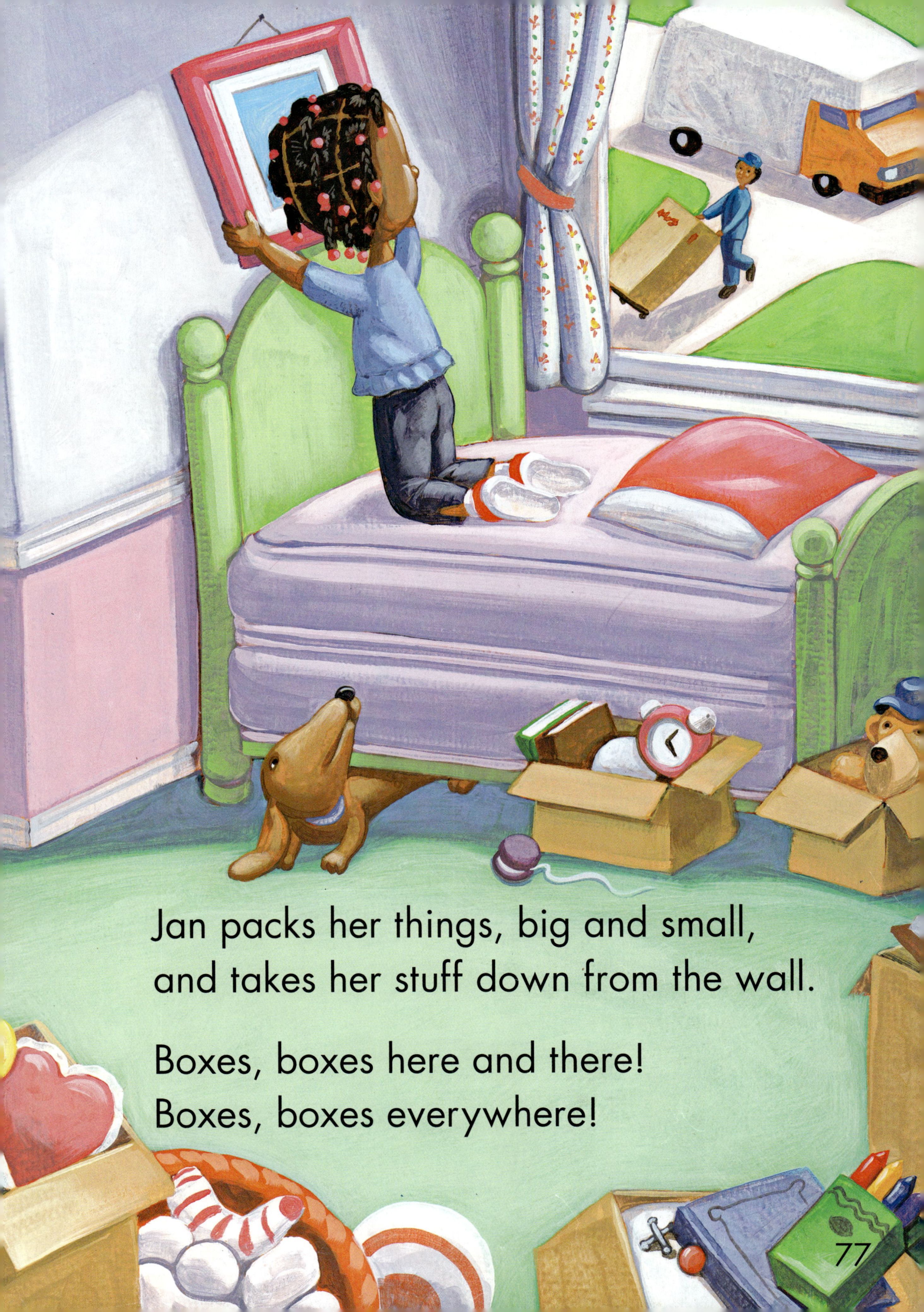

Jan packs her things, big and small,
and takes her stuff down from the wall.

Boxes, boxes here and there!
Boxes, boxes everywhere!

Our time in this home is at an end. Time for a new house, new school, new friends.

Everything is packed. It is time to go.
Jan takes a last look from the car window.

She sees horses, sheep, and lots of trees,
beautiful flowers and buzzing bees.

They stop for a picnic on the way.
Jan and her family eat and play.
It's a beautiful day with lots of sun.
Jan feels good. This trip is fun!

Cars and buses are everywhere.
People rush here, and people rush there.

There are lots of stores and very tall towers.
No more horses or tall yellow flowers.

Time for bed.
We have come a long way.
This is our new home.
We are here to stay.

New house, new school, and lots of change.
But Jan's little bed is still the same.
Some things are new. Some things change.
But the very best things are still the same.

Read Together

Think and Share

Talk About It What would you miss most if you were to move away from your home?

1. Use the pictures below to retell the story.
2. What is the big idea of this story? What did you learn about moving?
3. Did anything confuse you as you read? What did you do about it? How did that help?

Look Back and Write Look back at pages 82–83. How is Jan's new neighborhood different from her old one?

Meet the Author

Angela Shelf Medearis

Angela Medearis has moved to a new home many times. She says, "My father was in the Air Force. We moved almost every year!"

Ms. Medearis says to get better at reading, read as much as you can. "Put a book in the car. Keep a book in your backpack so you will always have something fun to do!"

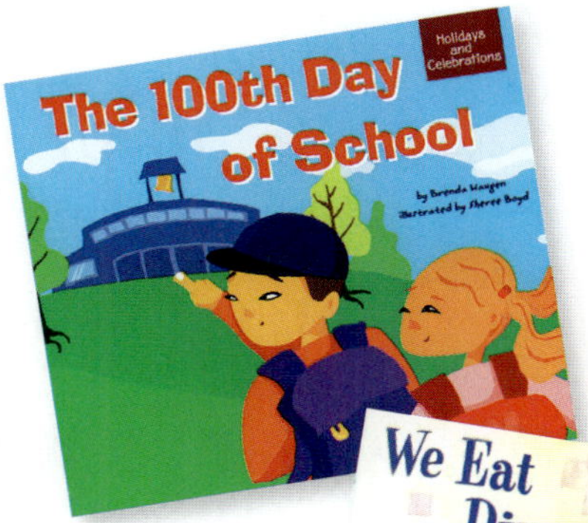

Read more books by Angela Shelf Medearis.

A Letter from Jan

Dear Hope,

I was sad when we drove away in our car. I liked our old house very much. But now I like my new home! We still have lots of boxes in the house.

I met more friends at school. They are very nice.

I hope you will come to see me.

Your friend,
Jan

This is for you.
It is my new home.

Read Together

Verbs That Do Not Add -s

Do not add **-s** to a verb that tells what two or more people, animals, or things do now.

Jan and her mother **pack** boxes.

Two people are packing, so we do not add **-s** to the word **pack.**

Two dogs **bark.**

Two dogs are barking, so we do not add **-s** to the word **bark.**

Write Using Verbs That Do Not Add -s

1. Write these sentences. Use the verbs that show more than one.

Jan and her friends (say, says) good-bye.

Mom and Dad (stop, stops) at the park.

2. Write a sentence that tells how Jan and her parents get to their new home. Circle the verb.

3. Write some sentences that tell what Mom and Dad do to make Jan feel at home in her new room. Circle the verbs.

Let's Talk About

Changes in Nature

Words to Read

afraid
read
soon
again
how
few

Read the Words

Frog was **afraid**. Toad **read** to him. **Soon** Frog went to sleep **again**.

"Now **how** can I get to sleep?" asked Toad. "I will **read** a **few** pages to myself."

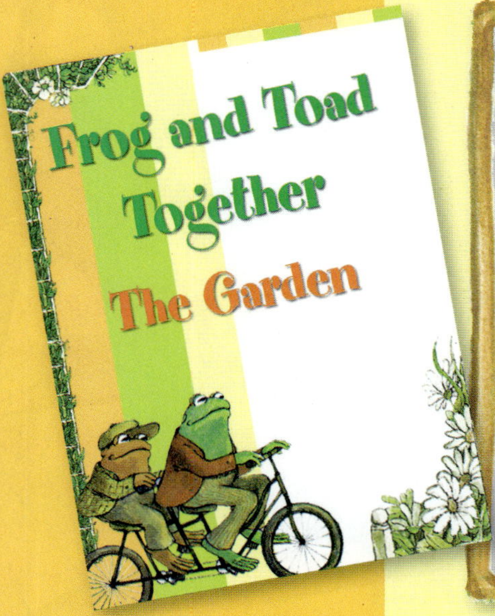

Genre: Animal Fantasy
In an animal fantasy, animals say and do things that people might say and do. Next you will read about two friends, Frog and Toad, who act very much like people.

Frog and Toad Together

by Arnold Lobel

The Garden

What do seeds need to grow?

Frog was in his garden.
Toad came walking by.

"What a fine garden you have, Frog,"
he said.

"Yes," said Frog. "It is very nice,
but it was hard work."

"I wish I had a garden," said Toad.

"Here are some flower seeds.
Plant them in the ground," said Frog,
"and soon you will have a garden."

"How soon?" asked Toad.

"Quite soon," said Frog.

Toad ran home.
He planted the flower seeds.

"Now seeds," said Toad, "start growing."

Toad walked up and down a few times.
The seeds did not start to grow.

Toad put his head close to the ground and said loudly,

"Now seeds, start growing!"

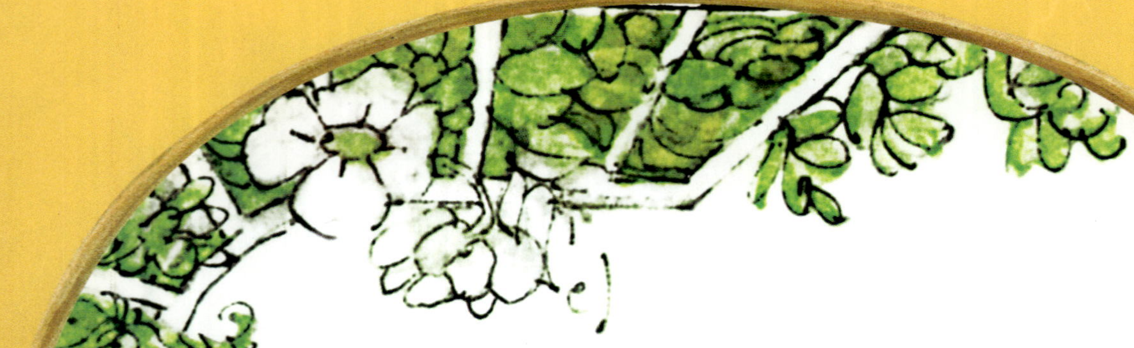

Toad looked at the ground again.
The seeds did not start to grow.

Toad put his head very close
to the ground and shouted,

"NOW SEEDS, START GROWING!"

Frog came running up the path.
"What is all this noise?" he asked.

"My seeds will not grow," said Toad.

"You are shouting too much," said Frog.
"These poor seeds are afraid to grow."

“My seeds are afraid to grow?” asked Toad.

“Of course,” said Frog.
“Leave them alone for a few days.
Let the sun shine on them,
let the rain fall on them.
Soon your seeds will start to grow.”

That night Toad looked out of his window.

"Drat!" said Toad. "My seeds have not started to grow. They must be afraid of the dark." Toad went out to his garden with some candles.

"I will read the seeds a story,"
said Toad. "Then they will not be afraid."

Toad read a long story to his seeds.

All the next day Toad
sang songs to his seeds.

And all the next day Toad
read poems to his seeds.

And all the next day Toad
played music for his seeds.

Toad looked at the ground.
The seeds still did not start to grow.

"What shall I do?" cried Toad.
"These must be the most frightened seeds in the whole world!"

Then Toad felt very tired, and he fell asleep.

"Toad, Toad, wake up," said Frog.
"Look at your garden!"

Toad looked at his garden.

Little green plants were coming up out of the ground.

"At last," shouted Toad, "my seeds have stopped being afraid to grow!"

"And now you will have a nice garden too," said Frog.

"Yes," said Toad, "but you were right, Frog. It was very hard work."

Read Together

Think and Share

Talk About It What was the funniest thing Toad did to get his seeds to grow? Read that part out loud.

1. Use the pictures below to retell the story.
2. What did you think about the story's ending? Tell about it.
3. What picture came to your mind when you read about Toad playing music for his plants? How did that help you?

Look Back and Write Look back at page 104. What advice does Frog give to Toad?

Meet the Author and Illustrator

Arnold Lobel

When Arnold Lobel first wrote about Frog and Toad, there were not many books for beginning readers that were fun to read. Mr. Lobel used easy words, and children love those good friends Frog and Toad!

As a boy, Mr. Lobel liked to draw silly animal pictures for his friends. When he grew up, he wrote and illustrated almost 100 books!

Read more stories about Frog and Toad.

Growing Plants

Do not be afraid to start a garden.
It is not hard. Read how.

1. Plant a few seeds.

2. Let the sun shine on them.

3. Water the seeds again and again.

Soon you will be growing
large plants.

1.

2.

3.

Read Together

Verbs for Now and the Past

Verbs can tell what happens now. Verbs can tell what happened in the past. Some verbs that tell about the past end with **-ed.**

Toad **plants** seeds. (now)

Toad **planted** seeds. (past)

Write Using Verbs for Now and the Past

1. Find and write a sentence from the story that tells about the past. Circle the verb that shows the past.

2. Write a sentence that tells about something you did yesterday. Use a verb that ends with **-ed** to show the past. Circle it.

3. Describe the helpful things that Toad did to get his seeds to grow. Use verbs that end with **-ed** to show the past. Circle the verbs.

Let's Talk About Changes in Nature

Words to Read

know
done
push
wait
visit

Read the Words

Let's find out about insects.

Do you **know** what's in here?

When the insect inside is **done** growing, it will **push** its way out.

What will it be?
Wait and see.
Then it will **visit** the garden.

Genre: Nonfiction
Nonfiction selections teach us about something in the real world. Next you will read about the life cycle of a caterpillar.

I'm a Caterpillar

by Jean Marzollo
illustrated by Judith Moffatt

How does a caterpillar grow and change?

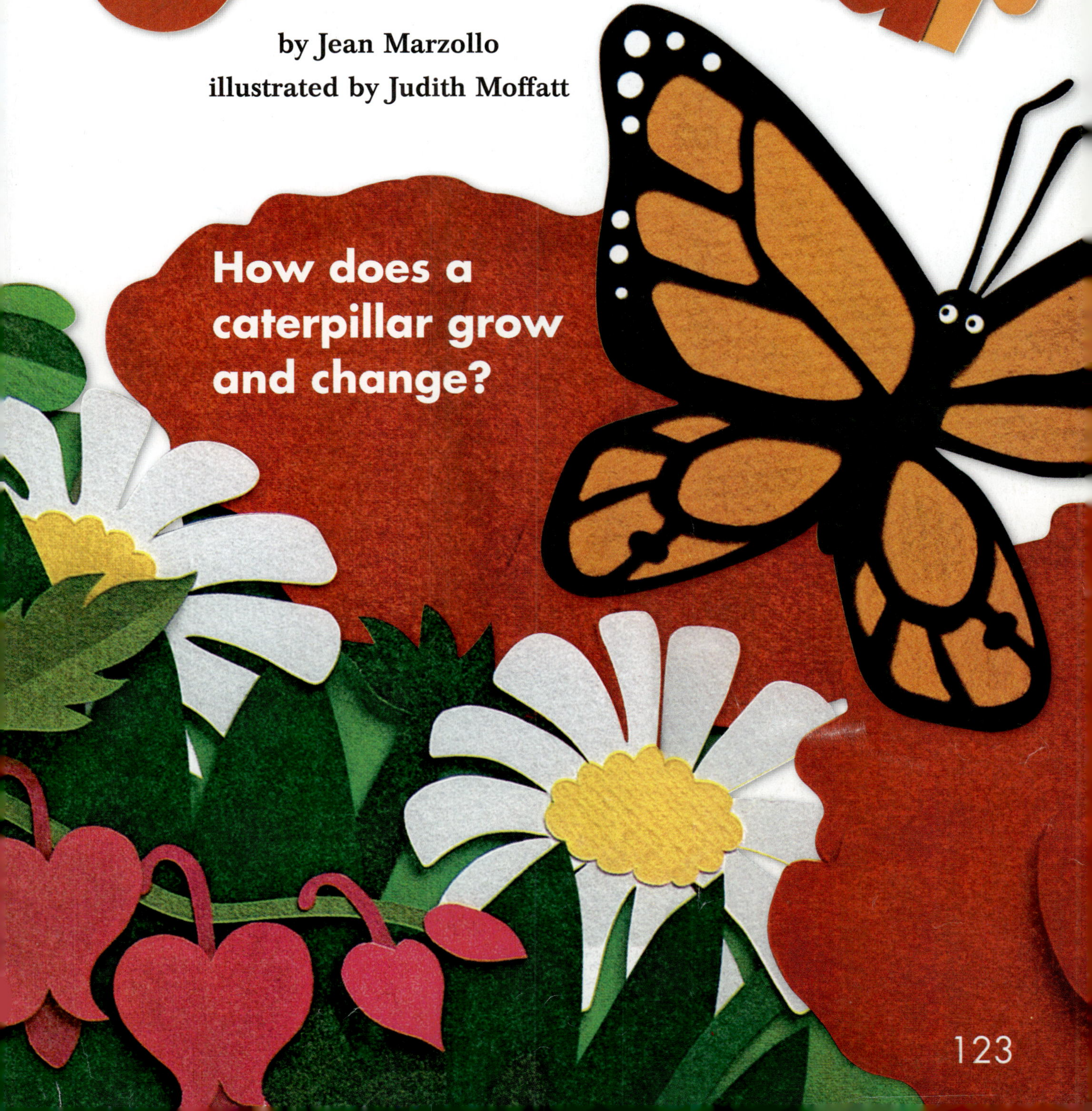

I'm a caterpillar. Munch. Crunch.
I'm getting bigger! Munch. Crunch.

Munch. Crunch. Munch. Crunch.
That's it. No more food. I'm done.

It's time to hang from a stem.

I wait,

and wait,

and wait.

I shiver.
I twist.
I split my skin!

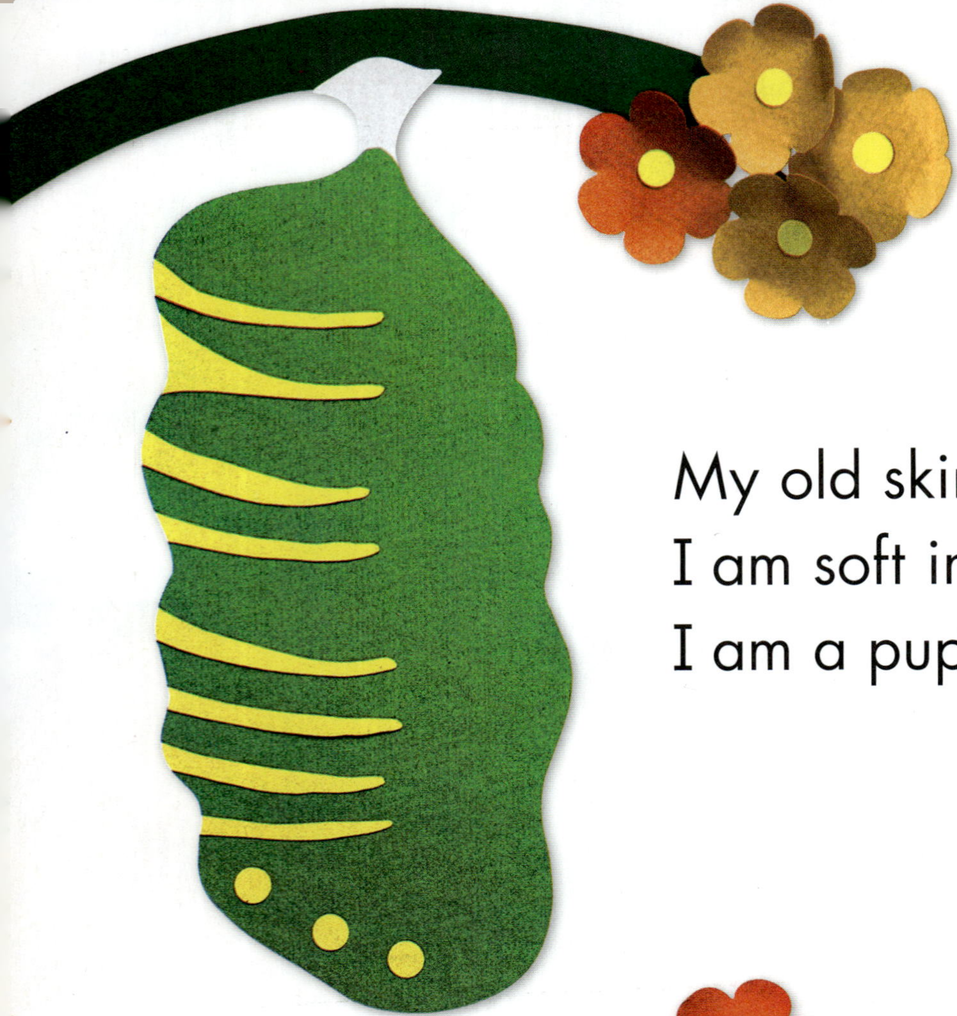

My old skin falls away.
I am soft inside.
I am a pupa.

I grow a shell
to protect the pupa.
I am now a chrysalis.

I keep changing.
Soon I'll come out.
What will I be?

A butterfly!

Push. Crack. Wow! I'm free!

My wings are all wet.

My wings dry off. They unfold.

Flap. Flap. Hey! I can fly! Ta-da!

I visit flowers. I drink nectar. Yum!

My mouth is like a straw.

Sip. Sip. Sip.

I have a mate. We visit many flowers.
We're not afraid of birds.
They know that we taste awful.

Soon I will lay my eggs.

The eggs have thin shells.

Baby caterpillars crawl out.

Hi! I'm a caterpillar.

Munch. Crunch.

What will happen to me next?
Do you know?

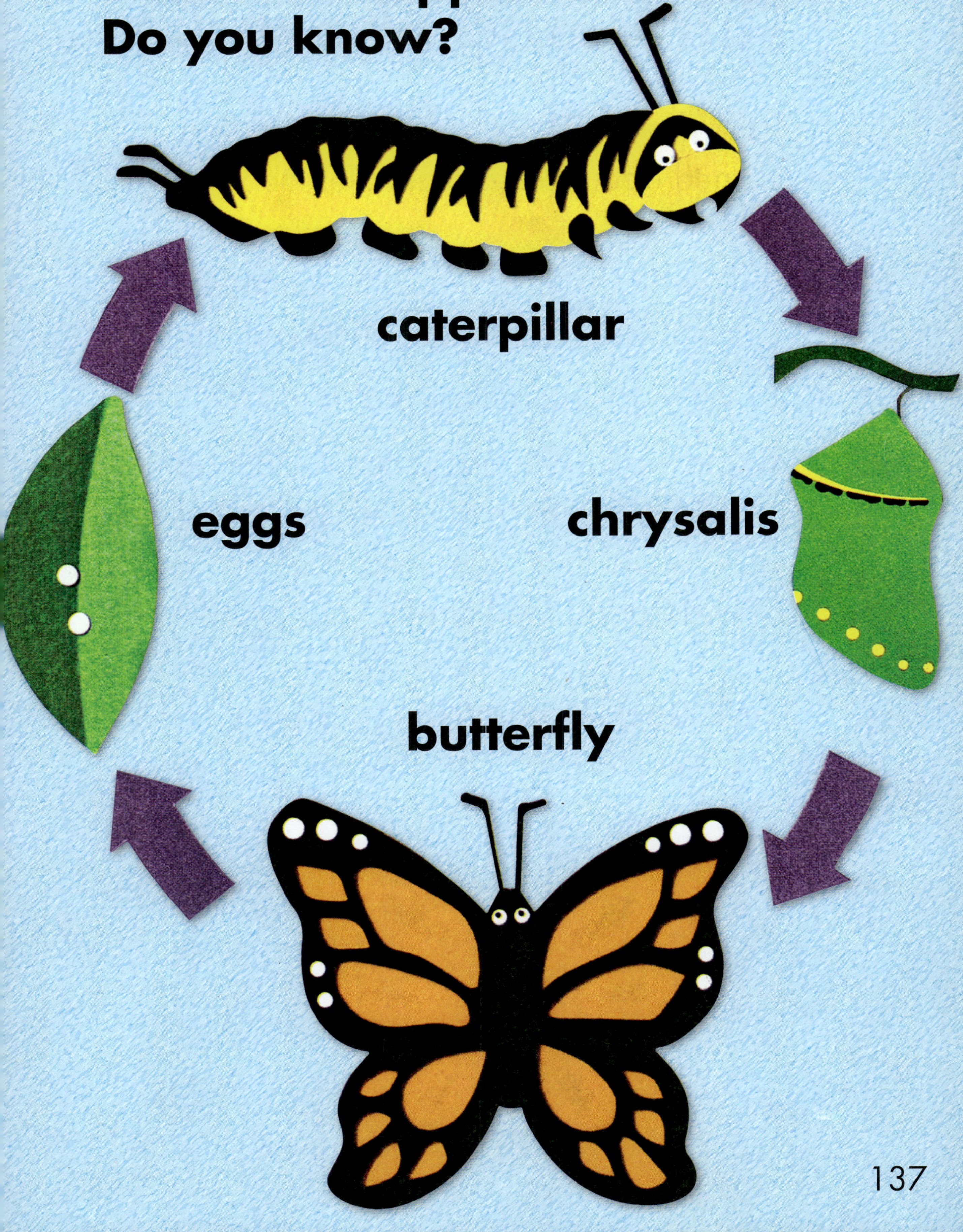

Read Together

Think and Share

Talk About It What is one thing you learned about caterpillars? Tell about it.

1. Use the pictures below to summarize what you learned about caterpillars.
2. Why do caterpillars eat so much?
3. The writer tells about caterpillars from little to big or from caterpillar to butterfly. How did that order help you read and understand the story?

Look Back and Write Look back at page 134. Why aren't butterflies afraid of birds?

Meet the Author

Jean Marzollo

Jean Marzollo was a high school teacher and a magazine editor. Now she has written more than 100 books for children! She writes about science, and she writes poetry, made-up stories, and *I Spy* books.

Ms. Marzollo likes to sew and work in her garden. She says writing is creative in the same way. It is hard and fun.

Read other books by Jean Marzollo.

My Computer

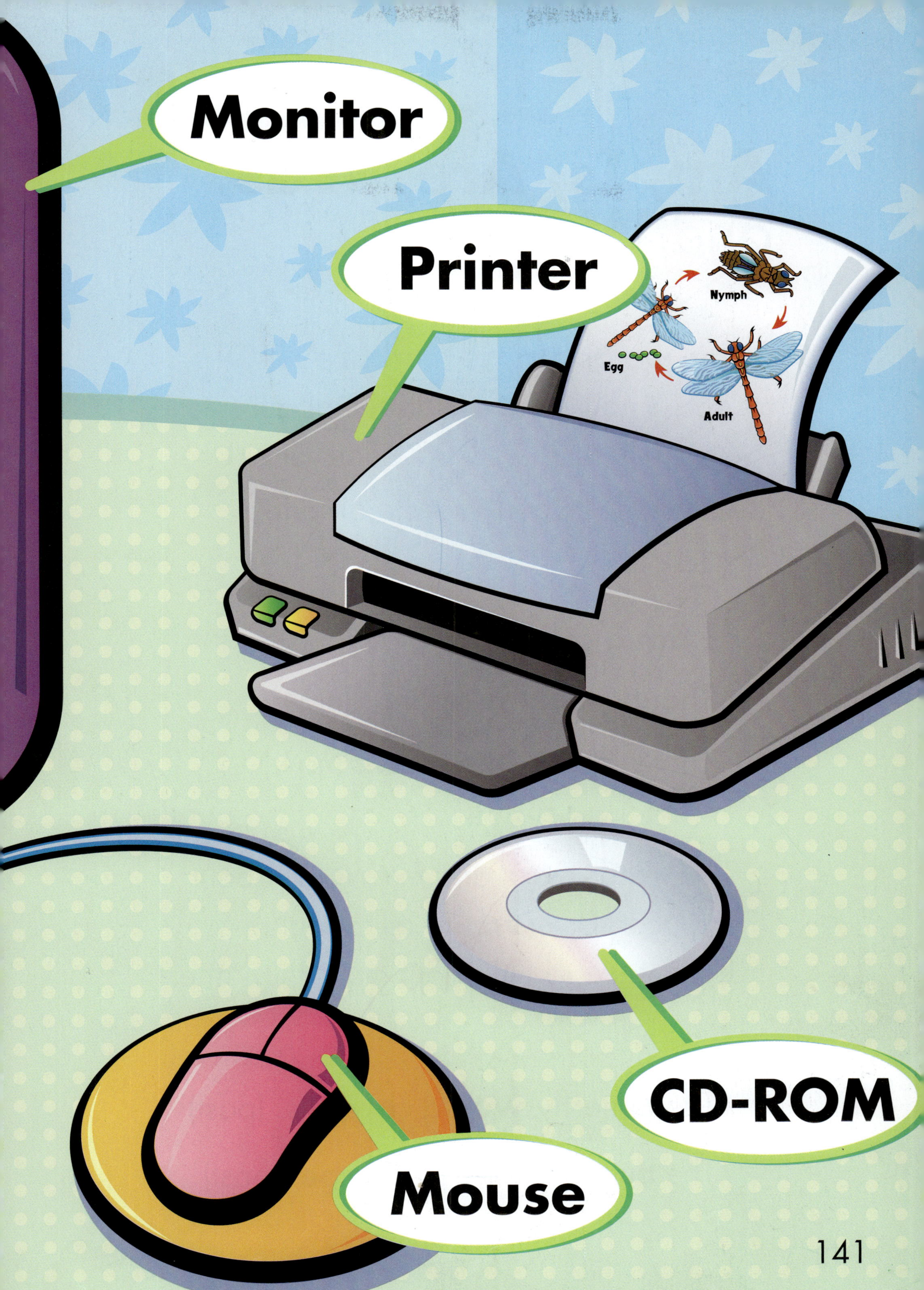
Monitor
Printer
Nymph
Egg
Adult
CD-ROM
Mouse

Read Together

Am, Is, Are, Was, and **Were**

The words **am, is,** and **are** tell about now. Use **am** to tell about yourself. Use **is** to tell about one. Use **are** to tell about more than one.

I **am** a caterpillar. (now)

That butterfly **is** resting. (now)

Those leaves **are** green. (now)

The words **was** and **were** tell about the past. Use **was** to tell about one. Use **were** to tell about more than one.

The butterfly **was** a chrysalis. (past)

The butterflies **were** orange. (past)

Write Using Am, Is, Are, Was, and Were

1. Write **Now** or **Past** to tell which each sentence tells about.

A butterfly was on the porch.
The caterpillars are on the branch.

2. Choose the correct verb. Then write each sentence.

I (was, were) in the garden.
They (is, are) watching the butterfly.

3. Write about something you see out the window. Use **am, is, are, was,** or **were** correctly.

Let's Talk About Changes in Nature

Words to Read

does
good-bye
before
won't
oh
right

Read the Words

"Does anyone know where Squirrel is?" asked Bear. "I want to say good-bye before my long nap. I won't see anyone for a while. Oh, I'm so sleepy! It is nap time right now."

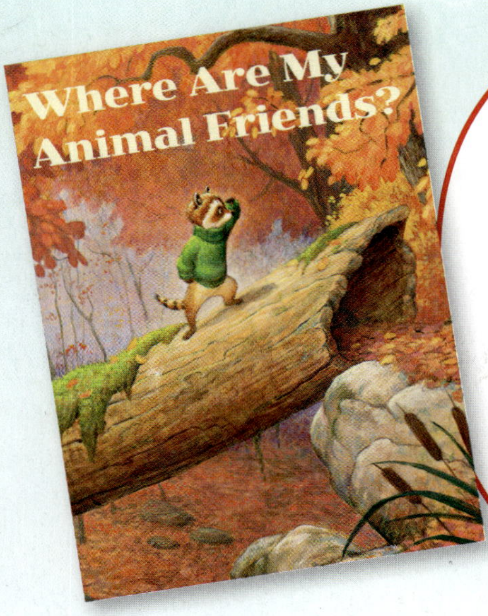

Genre: Play
A play is a story that is written to be acted out. Next you can read and then act out a play about animal friends who get ready for winter.

Where Are My Animal Friends?

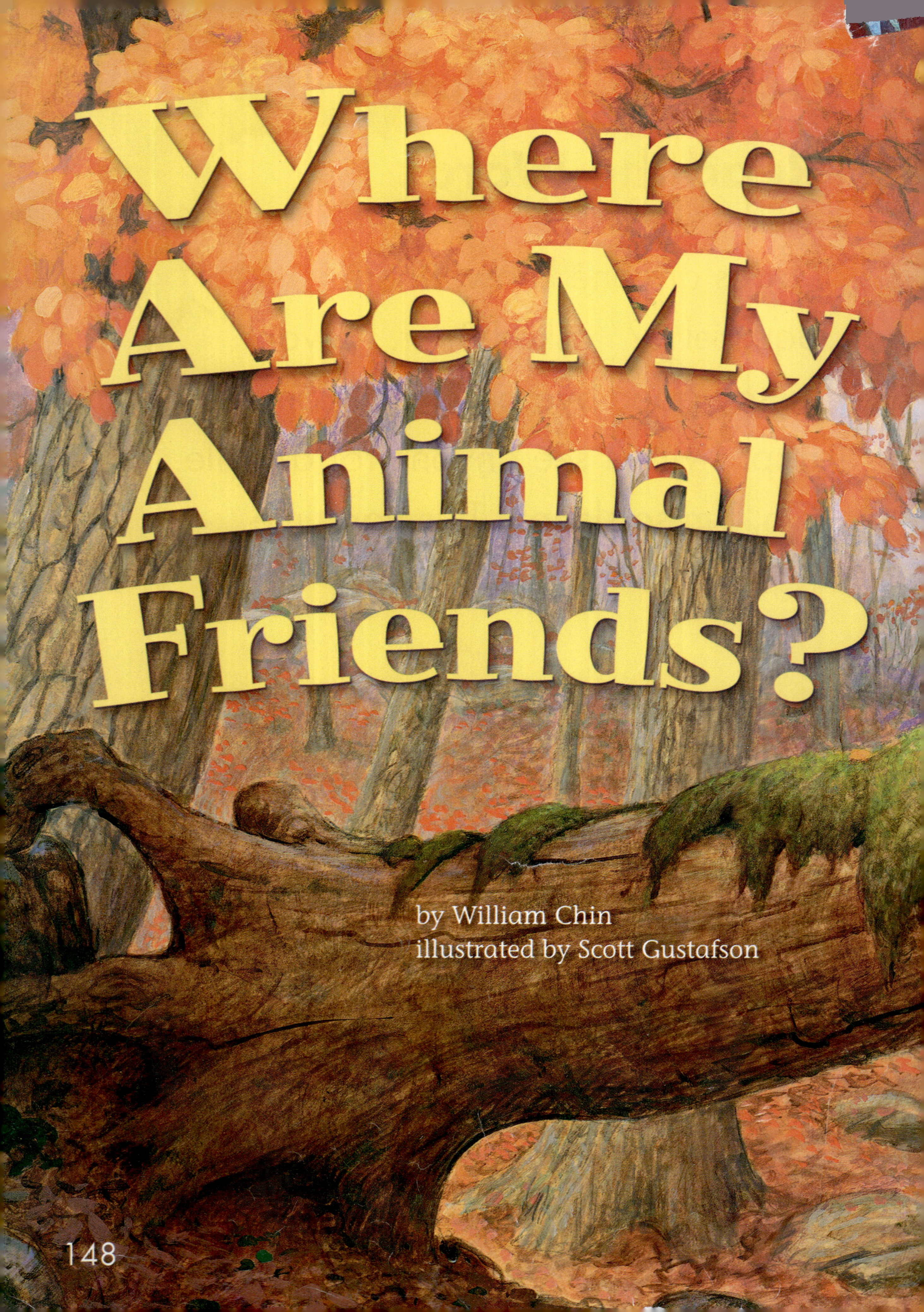

by William Chin
illustrated by Scott Gustafson

Where do animals go when the days turn cold?

Characters

Raccoon

Goose

Bear

Hummingbird

Squirrel

Hello, Goose! Why are you shivering?

The forest is chilly, Raccoon.
The days are shorter now. And it's getting colder every day.

Then we don't have much time to find our friends.

You're right, Raccoon. Let's look for Caterpillar.

Caterpillar lives in this tree.
But where are all the leaves?

Many of them are on the ground.
Where is Caterpillar?

Look, here comes the smallest bird in the forest. Hello, Hummingbird! Have you seen Caterpillar?

Oh, yes. Caterpillar is right here.

That's not Caterpillar! Caterpillar is long. This thing is not long.

Our friend Caterpillar moves a lot. This thing does not move at all.

But Caterpillar is inside. He became a chrysalis.

Then we won't see Caterpillar until spring when he'll be a butterfly.

Well, I'm glad you will be here for the winter.

Oh, no, Raccoon. I can't stay. I must fly away to where it is warm. Hummingbird does too.

Yes, we must go now.

Oh, my! I am the saddest raccoon in the forest. Will you come back?

Yes, we'll be back in the spring. Good-bye, Raccoon!

Good-bye, Goose! Good-bye, Hummingbird! I will see if Bear is at home.

Hello, Bear!

Hello, Raccoon. Is it spring yet?

No, Bear. It will be winter before it is spring. Why are you sleeping?

I ate and ate all summer. Now I am fatter than before, and I don't need to eat. I will sleep a long time. I won't budge until spring.

Oh, no! All my friends
are going away!

Pardon me, but I'm sleepy.
Good night, Raccoon!

Good night, Bear. But who will be my friend? Oh, here comes Squirrel.

Hello, Raccoon. Where is everyone?

Goose flew away, and so did Hummingbird. Caterpillar is now a chrysalis, and Bear is sleeping for the winter. Are you going away too?

Oh, no. I will stay here all winter.
I have a warm nest and lots of food.
Will you play with me?

Yes, Squirrel! Let's race to the edge of the forest and back!

Read Together

Put on a Play!

What you will need:

Costumes

Costumes can be simple or fancy.

Props

One prop you will need for this play is a chrysalis. Will you need anything else?

Scenery

Simple sets can show that the play is set in a forest in the fall.

An Audience

Practice your parts. Then ask another class to come to the play!

Read Together

Think and Share

Talk About It Only one of Raccoon's friends will stay for the winter. What do you think they will do together all winter long?

1. Use the pictures below to retell the story.
2. What does Bear do before he goes to sleep for the winter?
3. What did you already know about caterpillars that helped you as you read?

Look Back and Write Look back at pages 151 and 152. How do the animals know that winter is coming to the forest?

Meet the Author

William Chin

William Chin likes the winter. He lives in Chicago, where it gets cold in winter. His daughter is a figure skater. He and his wife skate too.

Mr. Chin sang in musicals in school. Now he is a choir director. He works with a children's choir. He is also a conductor for the Chicago Symphony Chorus.

Here are more books about winter.

Read Together

This Tooth

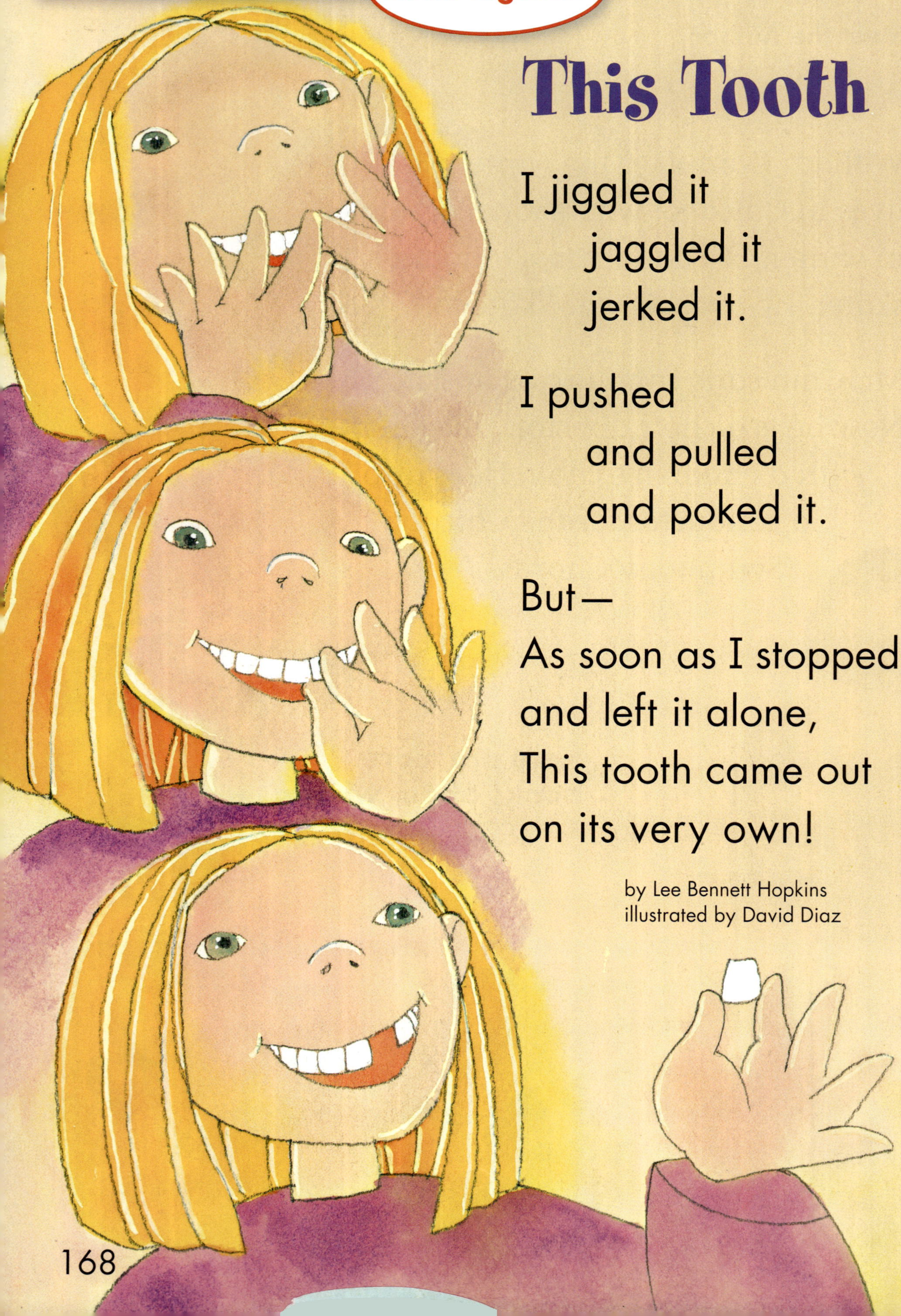

I jiggled it
jaggled it
jerked it.

I pushed
and pulled
and poked it.

But—
As soon as I stopped,
and left it alone,
This tooth came out
on its very own!

by Lee Bennett Hopkins
illustrated by David Diaz

Tommy

I put a seed into the ground
And said, "I'll watch it grow."
I watered it and cared for it
As well as I could know.

One day I walked in my back yard,
and oh, what did I see!
My seed had popped itself right out,
Without consulting me.

by Gwendolyn Brooks
illustrated by David Diaz

Read Together

Where Do Fish Go in Winter?

When lakes turn to ice
And are covered with snow,
What becomes of the fish
Who are living below?

It's not so exciting
Down under the ice,
But fish find it restful
And really quite nice.

It's dark and it's cold,
But the water's not frozen.
In fact, it's just perfect
For fish to repose in.

They breathe very little.
Their swimming gets slower.
Each fish makes his heart rate
Go lower and lower.

And except for occasional
Lake bottom treats,
The whole winter long
The fish hardly eats.

by Amy Goldman Koss
illustrated by Laura J. Bryant

Read Together

Contractions with Not

A **contraction** is a short way to put two words together. A **verb** and the word **not** can be put together to make a contraction. An **apostrophe (')** is used in place of the letter **o** in the word **not.**

are + not = **aren't**

has + not = **hasn't**

did + not = **didn't**

is + not = **isn't**

do + not = **don't**

was + not = **wasn't**

does + not = **doesn't**

were + not = **weren't**

Write Using Contractions with Not

1. Write a sentence from the play that uses a contraction with *not*. Circle the contraction.

2. Write a sentence using a contraction from page 172. Circle the contraction. Write the sentence again using the two words in place of the contraction.

3. Which season is not your favorite? Write about it. Use two or more contractions with *not*. Circle them.

UNIT 3 Wrap-Up

Read Together

Growing Me

connect to **WRITING**

How have you changed since you began first grade? Make a picture. Show one way you changed. Write a sentence about it.

How Seeds Grow and Change

connect to **SCIENCE**

Plant some seeds. Radish seeds or grass seeds are good. Water the seeds. Then put them in the sun. Watch them for a few days. Make a picture. Show what happens. Write what the seeds need to grow.

Step by Step

connect to **SCIENCE**

Make a caterpillar from five big paper circles. Think about how a caterpillar grows. Show one step on each circle.

Answering Questions

Where can you find the answers to questions you read?

In the Book

Sometimes the answers are RIGHT THERE in the book. You can put your finger right on the answer.

Right There

1. First, read the text.
2. Next, read the question and all the answer choices.
3. Then, look back at the text to find the answer.

Try It!

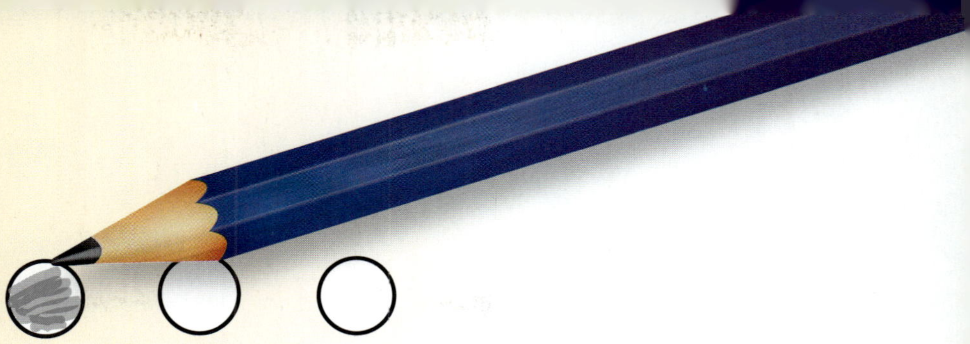

You might read this text and this question:

Jan has to move away. Jan feels sad. She wants to stay in her old house. She wants to see her old friends.

1 How does Jan feel?

○ happy

○ sad

○ cold

Look back at the text.
The answer is RIGHT THERE.

Put your finger on the answer in the text. Then put your finger on the right answer to the question.

Glossary

Bb

beautiful If something is **beautiful,** it is very pretty to see or hear. After the rain stopped, it became a **beautiful,** sunny day.

boy A **boy** is a male child. A **boy** grows up to be a man.

Cc

caterpillar A **caterpillar** is an insect that looks like a furry worm. **Caterpillars** turn into moths or butterflies.

chrysalis A caterpillar becomes a **chrysalis** when it grows a hard shell around itself.

crawl When you **crawl**, you move on your hands and knees or with your body close to the ground. Worms, snakes, and lizards **crawl.**

Ff

father A **father** is a man who has a child or children.

feather

feather A **feather** is one of the light, soft things that cover a bird's body.

flew The bird **flew** away. We **flew** to New York in an airplane.

Gg

goose A **goose** is a large bird with a long neck. A **goose** looks like a duck but is larger.

grew The grass **grew** very fast from all the rain.

ground The **ground** is the soil or dirt on the surface of the Earth. The **ground** was rocky.

Hh

head Your **head** is the top part of your body or the front part of most animals' bodies. Your **head** is where your eyes, ears, nose, mouth, and brain are.

Mm

mother A **mother** is a woman who has a child or children.

move To **move** means to change the place where you live. We live in the city now, but my parents want to **move** to the country.

Nn

night **Night** is the time between evening and morning.

Pp

precious

precious **Precious** means having great value. Mom's ring is very **precious** to her.

pupa The **pupa** is the form of an insect while it is changing from a wormlike larva into an adult.

Rr

raccoon

raccoon A **raccoon** is a small animal with thick fur. Its tail is long and has rings of a different color. **Raccoons** look for food at night.

rain

rain **Rain** is the water that falls in drops from the clouds. The **rain** made us all wet as we walked home from school.

Ss

shiver To **shiver** is to shake.

shouted When you have **shouted,** you have called out or yelled loudly. She **shouted** for help.

shouting

shouting When you are **shouting,** you are calling or yelling.

spring **Spring** is the season of the year between winter and summer. **Spring** is the season when plants begin to grow.

sunset **Sunset** is the time when the sun is last seen in the evening.

sunset

Tt

tower

tower A **tower** is a tall building or part of a building. A **tower** may stand alone or may be a part of a church, castle, or other building.

toys **Toys** are things to play with. Dolls, blocks, and teddy bears are **toys.**

toys

Ww

warm If something is **warm,** it is more hot than cold. The water is **warm** enough to swim in. He sat in the **warm** sunshine.

window A **window** is an opening in a wall or roof. A **window** lets in light or fresh air.

window

Tested Words

An Egg Is an Egg

always
become
day
everything
nothing
stays
things

Ruby in Her Own Time

any
enough
ever
every
own
sure
were

Jan's New Home

away
car
friends
house
our
school
very

Frog and Toad Together

afraid
again
few
how
read
soon

Tested Words

I'm a Caterpillar

done
know
push
visit
wait

Where Are My Animal Friends?

before
does
good-bye
oh
right
won't

Acknowledgments

Text

Page 14: From *An Egg Is an Egg* by Nicki Weiss, copyright © 1990 by Monica J. Weiss. Used by permission G.P. Putnam's Sons, A Division of Penguin Young Readers Group, A Member of Penguin Group (USA) Inc., 345 Hudson Street, New York, NY 10014. All rights reserved.

Page 40: *Ruby in Her Own Time* by Jonathan Emmett, illustrated by Rebecca Horry. Text copyright © 2003 by Jonathan Emmett, illustration copyright © 2003 by Rebecca Harry. Reprinted by permission of Scholastic Inc.

Page 96: "The Garden" from *Frog and Toad Together* by Arnold Lobel. Used by permission of HarperCollins Publishers.

Page 122: From *I'm A Caterpillar* by Jean Marzollo, illustrated by Judith Moffat. A Hello Science Reader! Book published by Cartwheel Books/Scholastic Inc. Text copyright © 1997 by Jean Marzollo, illustrations copyright © 1997 by Judith Moffat. Reprinted by permission. Hello Reader and Cartwheel Books are registered trademarks of Scholastic Inc.

Page 168: "This Tooth" by Lee Bennett Hopkins. Copyright © 1970 by Lee Bennett Hopkins. First appeared in *ME!*, published by Seabury Press. Reprinted by permission of Curtis Brown, Ltd.

Page 169: "Tommy" by Gwendolyn Brooks. Reprinted by consent of Brooks Permission.

Page 170: "Where Do Fish Go In Winter?", from *Where fish Go in Winter And Other great Mysteries* by Amy Goldman Koss, copyright © 1987, by Amy Goldman Koss, text. Illustrated by Laura J. Bryant, copyright © 2002 by Laura J. Bryant, illustrations. Used by permission of Dial Books for Young Readers, A Division of Penguin Young Readers Group, A Member of Penguin Group (USA) Inc., 345 Hudson Street, New York, NY 10014. All rights reserved.

Illustrations

Cover: Daniel Moreton

4-9 Julia Woolf

11, 14, 16-25, 27 Nicki Weiss

14-38, 62-63, 68-69 Rebecca Harry

24 Patrick Benson

30-33 Mary Bono

68 Steven Mach

72-85 Don Tate

92-117 Arnold Lobel

118-132 Judy Moffatt

150-164 Scott Gustafson

164-165 Courtesy David Diaz

171 Laura J Bryant

174-175 Julia Woolf

Photographs

Every effort has been made to secure permission and provide appropriate credit for photographic material. The publisher deeply regrets any omission and pledges to correct errors called to its attention in subsequent editions.

Unless otherwise acknowledged, all photographs are the property of Scott Foresman, a division of Pearson Education.

Photo locators denoted as follows: Top (T), Center (C), Bottom (B), Left (L), Right (R), Background (Bkgd).

10 ©Ariel Skelley/Corbis

11 (T) ©Kevin Dodge/Masterfile Corporation, (BL) ©Michael Newman/PhotoEdit

29 ©Nicki Weiss

36 (BC) Digital Vision, (BL) ©Jim Craigmyle/Corbis, (BR) ©Tom & Dee Ann McCarthy/Corbis

37 (BL) ©Royalty-Free/Corbis, (BR) ©Janette Beckman/Corbis

64 (CR, CL) ©Ariel Skelley/Corbis

69 (CL) Getty Images, (TR) Tom & Dee Ann McCarthy/Corbis

92 ©Frank Cruz/Index Stock Imagery

93 (TL) ©Ben Weaver/Getty Images, (CR) ©Roger Ball/Corbis

114 Dave King/©DK Images

115 (CL) ©D. Boone/Corbis, (BL) ©William Taufic/Corbis

118 (CC) ©John Isaac/Getty Images, (CL, BC, CR) ©DK Images

119 (TL, TR, CC) ©DK Images, (TC) Frank Greenaway/©DK Images

121 (TR) ©John Mason (JLMO)/Ardea, (CC) ©Richard Cummins/Corbis

144 ©Ted Horowitz/Corbis

145 (T) ©LWA-Dann Tardif/Corbis, (C) ©James L. Amos/Corbis, (B) ©Carol Fuegi/Corbis

178 (TL) Rubberball Productions, (B) Digital Vision

179 (TR) Getty Images, (BL) Hemera Technologies

180 Hemera Technologies

181 (BC) Getty Images, (TR) Rubberball Productions

182 (TR) Hemera Technologies, (CR) ©Royalty-Free/Corbis, (BL) Ghislain & Marie David de Lossy/Image Bank/Getty Images

184 (L, CC, CL) Hemera Technologies, (CR, TR) Getty Images

185 (C) Getty Images

Glossary

The contents of this glossary have been adapted from *First Dictionary*. Copyright © 2000, Pearson Education, Inc.

Reading
STREET

Reading STREET

Grade 1

Reading/Language Arts

Tennessee

Reading and Writing Accomplishments

Standard 1

Reading Accomplishments
Content Standard 1.0

The student will develop the reading and listening skills necessary for word recognition, comprehension, interpretation, analysis, evaluation, and appreciation of print and nonprint text.

1.1.01 Develop oral language.

a. Show evidence of expanding oral language through vocabulary growth.

b. Implement rules for conversation (e.g., raise hands, take turns, focus attention on speaker).

c. Understand, follow, and give oral directions.

d. Participate in group discussions.

e. Participate in creative responses to text (e.g., choral reading, discussion, and drama).

f. Respond to questions from teacher and other group members.

g. Begin to narrate a personal story.

h. Dramatize or retell what has been learned, heard, or experienced.

i. Use familiar texts for recitations.

1.1.02 Develop listening skills.

a. Listen attentively to speaker for specific information.

b. Use appropriate listening skills (e.g., do not interrupt, face speaker, ask questions).

c. Listen and respond to a variety of media (e.g., books, audio tapes, videos).

d. Recognize the difference between formal and informal languages.

e. Understand and follow simple, three-step oral directions.

1.1.03 Demonstrate knowledge of concepts of print.

a. Understand that printed materials provide information.

b. Demonstrate directionality by reading left to right and top to bottom.

c. Track print when being read to aloud.

d. Read and explain own writings and drawings.

e. Identify parts of a book (e.g., title page, table of contents).

f. Recognize that groups of words make sentences.

g. Understand punctuation (e.g., period, question mark).

1.1.04 Develop and maintain phonemic awareness.

a. Recognize words that begin with the same sounds.

b. Recognize words that end with the same sounds.

c. Identify rhyming words.

d. Blend sounds together to form one-syllable words.

e. Segment one-syllable words into sounds.

f. Change targeted sounds to modify or change words.

g. Show awareness of syllables by clapping, counting, or moving objects.

1.1.05 Develop and use decoding strategies.

a. Use knowledge of letter-sound correspondence knowledge and structural analysis to decode grade-appropriate words.

b. Decode phonetically regular, one-syllable words.

c. Use decoding strategies, such as sounding out words, comparing similar words, breaking words into smaller words, and looking for word parts (e.g., compound words, word families, blends, and digraphs).

d. Apply long and short vowel rules when decoding.

e. Begin to decode unknown words automatically.

1.1.06 Read to develop fluency, expression, accuracy, and confidence.

a. Begin to read orally with accuracy and confidence using appropriate pacing, intonation, and expression.

b. Reflect punctuation of written text while reading orally.

c. Participate in guided oral readings.

d. Demonstrate the automatic recognition of high-frequency words.

e. Read with increasing fluency and confidence from a variety of texts through paired readings, shared reading, choral reading, teacher-led reading, and reading from tapes.

f. Read independently daily.

g. Recite familiar texts to develop fluency, expression, accuracy, and confidence.

1.1.07 Develop and extend reading vocabulary.

a. Build vocabulary by listening to literature, participating in discussions, and reading self-selected texts.

b. Build vocabulary through frequent read alouds.

c. Participate in shared reading.

d. Manipulate word families, word walls, and word sorts.

e. Match oral words to written words.

f. Determine the meaning of unfamiliar words by using a picture dictionary, picture clues, context clues, and structural analysis.

g. Add endings to base words (e.g., *-s, -ed, -es, -ing*).

h. Identify simple abbreviations.

1.1.08 Develop and use prereading strategies.

a. Develop a purpose for listening/reading.

b. Participate in activities to build background knowledge to derive meaning from text.

c. Make predictions about text.

d. Use illustrations to preview text.

1.1.09 Use active comprehension strategies to derive meaning while reading and check for understanding after reading.

a. Derive meaning while reading by

1. asking questions about text.
2. recognizing errors in reading as they occur and self-correct.
3. participating in discussions about text and relating to personal experiences.
4. creating graphic organizers (e.g., charts, lists).
5. predicting and adjusting outcomes during read alouds.

b. Check for understanding after reading by

1. recalling three- to four-step sequence of events.
2. retelling stories in their own words using sequencing words (i.e. *first, next, last*).
3. drawing conclusions based on what has been read.
4. recognizing main idea in pictures, picture books, and texts.

1.1.10 Introduce informational skills to facilitate learning.

a. Recognize the family and community as sources of information.

b. Recognize a variety of print items as sources of information (e.g. books, magazines, maps, charts, and graphs).

c. Recognize sources of information (e.g., books, maps, graphs, charts).

d. Use graphic organizers to aid in understanding material from informational text (e.g., charts, graphs, web).

e. Visit libraries to use and view appropriate material.

1.1.11 **Develop skills to facilitate reading to learn in a variety of content areas.**

a. Begin to develop content-specific vocabulary.

b. Use text features to locate information (e.g., maps, charts, illustrations, and table of contents).

1.1.12 **Read independently for a variety of purposes. (At this level, the student will explore as an emergent reader.)**

a. Read for literary experience.

b. Read to gain information.

c. Read to perform a task.

d. Read for enjoyment.

e. Read to expand vocabulary.

f. Read to build fluency.

1.1.13 **Experience various literary and media genres.**

a. Read and view various literary (e.g., picture books, storybooks, fairy tales, poetry, lyrics to songs) and media (e.g., illustrations, the arts, films, videos) genres.

b. Explore nonfiction.

c. Identify characters, events, and settings in print and nonprint text.

d. Recognize main character(s) in print and nonprint text.

e. Determine whether a selection is real or fantasy.

f. Recognize rhyme in Mother Goose and other rhyming books.

g. Retell a story in correct sequence (e.g., using books, videos, films).

h. Determine the problem in a story and discover its solution through classroom discussion.

1.1.14 Develop and maintain a motivation to read.

a. Visit libraries/media centers and regularly check out materials.

b. Share storybooks, poems, newspapers, and environmental print.

c. Explore a wide variety of literature through read alouds, tapes, and independent reading.

d. Identify favorite stories, informational text, authors, and illustrators.

e. Engage in a variety of literacy activities voluntarily (e.g., self-select books and stories).

f. Choose to read as a leisure activity.

Standard 2

Writing Accomplishments
Content Standard 2.0

The student will develop the structural and creative skills of the writing process necessary to produce written language that can be read, presented to, and interpreted by various audiences.

1.2.01 Use a variety of prewriting strategies.

a. Brainstorm ideas with teacher and peers.

b. Draw pictures to generate ideas.

c. Construct graphic organizers (e.g., webs, charts, diagrams) as a small or large group to organize information.

d. Use a variety of sources to gather information.

1.2.02 Write for a variety of purposes.

a. Write to acquire and exhibit knowledge (e.g., word families, numbers, shapes, sensory words, and sentences).

b. Write to entertain (e.g., stories and poems).

c. Write to inform (e.g., write simple directions, journals, friendly letters).

1.2.03 Show evidence of drafting and revision with written work.

a. Compose first drafts using appropriate parts of the writing process with an emphasis on planning and self-correction.

b. Write in complete, coherent sentences.

c. Use descriptive words when writing.

d. Use temporary spelling to spell independently as necessary.

e. Arrange events in logical/sequential order when writing or dictating.

f. Participate in teacher-led experience stories.

g. Reread draft and delete extraneous information.

h. Vary sentence types.

1.2.04 Include editing before the completion of finished work.

a. Apply elements of language (e.g., end marks, capitalization) and use complete sentences when writing and editing.

b. Use classroom resources (e.g., word walls, picture dictionaries, teacher, peers, appropriate technology, student-generated word books) to support the writing process.

c. Use knowledge of letter sounds, word parts, and word segmentation to monitor and correct spelling.

d. Create readable documents with legible handwriting.

e. Identify words or phrases that could be added to clarify meaning after writing or dictating a story.

1.2.05 Evaluate own and others' writing.

a. Use a simple rubric to evaluate writing/pictures and group work (e.g., happy face, stickers).

b. Discuss and react to writing.

c. Review personal collection to determine progress.

1.2.06 Experience numerous publishing opportunities.

a. Prepare a variety of written work (e.g., published books, classroom books, experience stories).

b. Use technology to publish writing.

c. Share completed work.

d. Create individual and classroom books.

e. Incorporate illustrations and photographs.

1.2.07 Write narrative accounts.

a. Write simple stories.

b. Write short accounts of personal experiences.

c. Write group stories with a beginning, middle, and ending.

1.2.08 Write frequently across content areas.

a. Summarize concepts presented in science (e.g., illustration, dictating sentences, or composing simple sentences).

b. Write stories using concepts presented in social studies.

c. Write in math journals, create math stories, and write explanations for problem solving.

d. Participate in shared writings about the arts and class activities.

1.2.09 Write expressively using original ideas, reflections, and observations.

a. Write when given time, place, and materials.

b. Maintain, with teacher assistance, samples of writing and drawings that express opinions and judgments (e.g., portfolio, journals, student-made books).

c. Dictate stories (e.g., to tape recorder, to adult, to older student).

1.2.10 Write in response to literature.

a. Write different endings to a story.

b. Summarize a story using simple sentences and illustrations.

c. Create class books based on literature selections.

d. Create and/or use an illustration, sign, or rebus symbols to respond to literature.

1.2.11 Write in a variety of modes and genres.

a. Write friendly notes and messages.

b. Write stories.

c. Write in journals.

d. Write rhymes and poems.

Standard 3

Elements of Language Accomplishments
Content Standard 3.0

The student will use standard English conventions and proper spelling as appropriate to speaking and writing.

1.3.01 Demonstrate knowledge of standard English usage.

a. Use nouns appropriately (e.g., singular and plural, possessive).

b. Use verbs (action words) appropriately (e.g., tense and agreement with simple subject).

c. Use pronouns appropriately (e.g., subject and object agreement).

d. Use adjectives appropriately (e.g., vivid description words).

1.3.02 Demonstrate knowledge of standard English mechanics.

a. Capitalize the first word of a sentence, first and last names, pronoun *I,* and proper nouns.

b. Use correct punctuation at the end of simple declarative sentences and questions.

c. Identify and use contractions.

d. Write legibly in manuscript, using proper spacing between letters of a word and words of a sentence.

1.3.03 Demonstrate knowledge of standard English spelling.

a. Spell high-frequency words correctly.

b. Spell words correctly as appropriate to grade level.

c. Spell three- and four-letter short vowel words and phonetically spell sight words correctly.

d. Alphabetize words to the first letter.

e. Begin to develop dictionary skills through the use of a picture dictionary.

1.3.04 Demonstrate knowledge of correct sentence structure.

a. Use complete and coherent sentences when speaking.

b. Identify complete sentences.

c. Write a simple sentence.

d. Identify and correct incomplete sentences.

e. Combine two simple sentences into a compound sentence using the word *and.*

f. Identify statements and questions by noting ending punctuation when writing and intonation when speaking.

Reading
STREET
Grade 1

READING STREET